UNSOLVED!

by Marie Powell

Crabtree Publishing Company

www.crabtreebooks.com

Crabtree Publishing Company
www.crabtreebooks.com

Author: Marie Powell
Project Editor: Tim Cooke
Designer: Lynne Lennon
Picture Researcher: Andrew Webb
Picture Manager: Sophie Mortimer
Art Director: Keith Davis
Editorial Director: Lindsey Lowe
Children's Publisher: Anne O'Daly
Editor: Kelly Spence
Proofreader: Kathy Middleton
Cover Design: Margaret Amy Salter
**Production Coordinator and
    Prepress Technician:** Ken Wright
Print Coordinator: Margaret Amy Salter

Photographs
Cover:
Interior: Alamy: Ian Cowe 13, Interfoto 10; Australian Transport Safety Bureau: NASA/Blue Marble/A. Heneen 28; Blurry Photos: 23; Bridgeman Art Library: DeAgostini Picture Library/G. Dagli Orti 14; Corbis: Bettmann 20; Dreamstime: Tero hakala, 15; L'Union France: Laurent ERRERA 29; Library of Congress: 4, 6, 11, 22, 25, 26; Mary Evans Picture Library: 12; Robert Hunt Library: 24, British Museum/John White 16, J. Giletta 7, Henry Howe 16, NPG 9; Shutterstock: Simon Booth 27, Click Images 21, Amy Nichole Harris 5, Marek Stefunko 8; U.S. Airforce: Aero Icarus/Zurich 19; U. S. Federal Government: 18.

Every attempt to contact copyright holders has been made by the publisher.

Library and Archives Canada Cataloguing in Publication

Powell, Marie, author
    Unsolved! / Marie Powell.

(Mystery files)
Includes index.
Issued in print and electronic formats.
ISBN 978-0-7787-8073-1 (bound).--ISBN 978-0-7787-8077-9 (pbk.).--ISBN 978-1-4271-9970-6 (pdf).--ISBN 978-1-4271-9966-9 (html)

    1. History--Miscellanea--Juvenile literature. I. Title.

D21.3.P68 2015   j909   C2014-908109-X
                                      C2014-908110-3

Library of Congress Cataloging-in-Publication Data

Powell, Marie, 1958-
 Unsolved! / Marie Powell.
    pages cm. -- (Mystery files)
 Includes index.
 ISBN 978-0-7787-8073-1 (reinforced library binding : alkaline paper) -- ISBN 978-0-7787-8077-9 (paperback : alkaline paper) -- ISBN 978-1-4271-9970-6 (electronic PDF) -- ISBN 978-1-4271-9966-9 (electronic html)
1. Curiosities and wonders--Juvenile literature. 2. History--Miscellanea--Juvenile literature. 3. Biography--Miscellanea--Juvenile literature. I. Title.

 AG243.P66 2015
 030--dc23
                            2014046816

Crabtree Publishing Company
www.crabtreebooks.com   1-800-387-7650

Published in Canada
Crabtree Publishing
616 Welland Ave.
St. Catharines, ON
L2M 5V6

Published in the United States
Crabtree Publishing
PMB 59051
350 Fifth Avenue, 59th Floor
New York, New York 10118

Published by CRABTREE PUBLISHING COMPANY in 2015
Copyright © 2015 Brown Bear Books Ltd

Contents

Introduction

Unsolved mysteries are fascinating. People like to know why things happen and become worried if something does not appear to have an obvious explanation. Those events include sudden disappearances, cases of mistaken identity, and messages that can't be decoded. Some mysteries may eventually be solved, but others may never be fully explained.

Some of the world's great mysteries have remained unsolved for centuries. Others are more recent. The researchers who investigate these types of stories range from professional scientists and law enforcement agencies to mystery fans. Despite hours of work, however, most researchers fail to come up with logical answers.

The true fate of Princess Anastasia of Russia was argued about for decades.

Unsolved Mysteries

In this book, you will meet people who have
returned from the dead, escaped capture, or vanished
into thin air. Read about the woman who claimed
to be the long-lost daughter of the last Russian **tsar**,
the famous pilot Amelia Earhart who mysteriously
disappeared over the Pacific Ocean, and the lost
colony of Roanoke that vanished without a trace.

Why did people on Easter Island erect these giant stone heads?

Mystery words...

colony: a settlement started in a new country by people from another country

The Man in the IRON MASK

It is known that in the late 1670s a man was locked up alone in a French jail. His face was hidden by a mask, which was later referred to as an iron mask. His identity remains a mystery to this day.

The prisoner is known as the Man in the Iron Mask. He was imprisoned for 34 years until he died on November 19, 1703. People have made many guesses about his identity. Was he an English nobleman, the French playwright Molière, or Louis de Bourbon, an **illegitimate** son of King Louis XIV?

The masked prisoner had the same jailer for his entire imprisonment.

Mystery words...

illegitimate: born to parents who are not married

Some people believe the man was Ercole Matthioli, who was kidnapped and imprisoned by King Louis XIV. Other people think he was Eustache Dauger, a servant of Nicolas Fouquet, a finance minister.

Some people think the mask was not made of iron, but of black velvet. Others also believed that the prisoner was not allowed to speak or write—if he did, he would have been executed immediately.

In his best-selling novel *The Man in the Iron Mask* (1850), the French author Alexandre Dumas suggested the mysterious prisoner was King Louis XIV's twin brother. The book inspired a movie in 1929 and another in 1998.

The masked prisoner was held in a castle on the Île Sainte-Marguerite.

The Princes in the TOWER

When King Edward IV of England died in 1483, his brother Richard sent the king's two sons to the Tower of London to lodge there until the oldest son's coronation day. But Richard seized the throne, and the young boys disappeared. Their fate remains an unsolved mystery.

Prince Edward was 12 when his father died. He was king himself for only three months. After he and his nine-year-old brother Richard were sent to the Tower, their uncle Richard, Duke of Gloucester, had the princes declared illegitimate heirs. The duke was crowned King Richard III in June 1483.

Later that year, the young princes disappeared. Many people believe they were killed by Richard. In the 17th century, builders in the Tower found the bones of two children.

It would require royal approval to test the DNA of the bones found in the Tower.

Mystery File:
THE PRETENDERS

In 1487, a 10-year-old named Lambert Simnel claimed falsely to be Edward, the king of England. Four years later, a man named Perkin Warbeck declared he was Edward. He invaded England in 1497, and was captured and executed in 1499. Was he an imposter, or the rightful king?

A Hidden Code

In 1995, a man named Jack Leslau believed he had solved the mystery. He claimed the two princes were smuggled out of the Tower and grew up under new identities. The younger prince grew up to be John Clement, a famous doctor. The **historian** claimed to have cracked a hidden code in a painting of Clement. Clues include a message in Latin, reading "John, the rightful heir," and a fleur-de-lis, which was a symbol of the royal family.

Most people believe the young princes were murdered in the Tower.

Princess
ANASTASIA

In 1918, Russian Tsar Nicholas II and all of his family were murdered after the Russian Revolution. The Tsar's youngest daughter, Anastasia, was rumored to have survived the massacre. Several people later claimed to be the missing princess.

Anna Andersen claimed to be Anastasia until she died.

In 1922 a woman named Anna Andersen claimed to be the Grand Duchess Anastasia. At the time, Andersen was a patient in a mental hospital in Germany. Most people did not take her seriously. People who had known Anastasia and the Romanov family said she was an imposter. Andersen tried to prove her identity, but a German court did not believe her. By now, however, her claims had made her famous.

Mystery words...

DNA: a chemical code passed from parents to their children

End of the Story

In 1968, Andersen married an American professor. She lived in Virginia until she died in 1984. At the time of her death, most people believed she was really a Polish woman named Franziska Schanzkowska. In 1991, the remains of the Romanov family were found in a mass grave. Scientists compared Anna Andersen's **DNA** with that of the royal family. There was no match—final proof that Andersen was not related to the Romanovs.

Mystery File: DNA EVIDENCE

When the Romanov grave was found in 1991, the bodies of two children were missing. In 2007, another grave was found nearby. It held two bodies. DNA evidence identified them as the two missing members of the family, ending decades of speculation.

All five children, including Anastasia (left), died with their parents.

Flannan Isles
LIGHTHOUSE

The **Flannan Isles lighthouse** is located on a remote island off the east coast of Scotland. In December 1900, the three lighthouse keepers disappeared without a trace.

On December 26, 1900, Joseph Moore sailed out to the Flannan Isles to take over from one of the keepers. When his ship neared the island, the lighthouse lamp was out. The captain blew a whistle and fired a rocket, but there was no response.

Moore landed and went to the lighthouse. He found the clocks stopped, the beds empty, and the great lamp ready to be lit.

A staircase allowed supplies to be carried up to the lighthouse.

Today, the lighthouse still warns ships to steer clear of the rocks around the Flannan Islands.

The keepers' oilskin coats and boots were missing. That suggested they had gone outside during a storm and had never returned.

The Sailors' Theory

The ship's captain sent a **telegram** to the mainland. He reported that he believed the men had been blown off the cliffs and drowned. After his report, two more ships reported that the lighthouse lamp had been out nearly two weeks earlier when they had sailed near the island during a fierce storm.

Mystery File: WHAT HAPPENED?

There are many theories about what happened. Perhaps the three men were swept away by a wave or killed each other in an argument. Superstitious people think they were taken by spirits. The lighthouse log mentions nothing out of the ordinary, so the mystery remains.

Mystery words...

telegram: a long-distance message sent by telegraph

RONGORONGO

Tablets found on remote Easter Island in the southeastern Pacific Ocean are carved with strange writing—but no one knows what they say because the script has never been decoded. Perhaps it holds the secrets of the island's famous statues.

Easter Island is the most remote island in the world. Its closest neighbors are 1,290 miles (2,075 km) away. When European explorers visited in the 1700s, they found only 3,000 people living on the island. It was clear, however, that a larger population had once lived there. The people had vanished leaving behind more than 600 huge heads carved from stone. The purpose of the stone heads remains a puzzle. One theory is that they represented the islanders' ancestors.

Rongorongo was carved on pieces of wood as well as into rocks.

An Unusual Script

Rongorongo, as the writing is known, was carved on rocks and wooden tablets. It uses a system of pictures, or **hieroglyphs**. They run from right to left and then left to right. The script does not resemble any other script. When Europeans arrived, the Easter Islanders still copied Rongorongo as a ritual, but did not know its meaning. All modern attempts to decode it have failed.

Another old tablet waiting to reveal its mysteries comes from Phaistos in Greece. Made during the Bronze Age, the clay disk shows 45 signs that occur more than 200 times each, like a chorus or hymn. Theories suggest it may be a prayer to a goddess.

The islanders carved huge statues that seem to watch over their territory.

Lost Colony of
ROANOKE

One of the first colonies of English settlers in North America was founded on an island off North Carolina. It was named Roanoke. A few years later it was found deserted. The only clue to the fate of the settlers was a mysterious word carved into a tree—Croatoan. No other sign of the colonists was ever found.

Virginia Dare, the first English settler born in America, is shown being baptized at Roanoke.

Mystery File:
NEW EVIDENCE

In 2013, archeologists studied old maps and used a satellite **survey** to look for land formations that may show signs of early settlement. From this, they think they have found signs the Roanoke colonists may have moved farther west.

John White drew this map of the Roanoke region in the 1580s.

In August 1587 the colony's leader, John White, sailed to England. He left over 100 colonists behind. When he returned three years later, the people had vanished. Only the word CROATOAN remained.

The Missing Settlers

White believed the colonists had moved to the neighboring island, Croatoan. However, there was no trace of them there either. Some people think the colonists may have died of disease, joined with local tribes, or been killed by them.

Mystery words...

satellite: a communications device that orbits the Earth

D.B. COOPER

In 1971, **D.B.** Cooper hijacked an airplane. He demanded money, then jumped from the plane with a parachute. In 1980, some of the money was found. What happened to Cooper remains a mystery.

A BULLETIN FROM THE F.B.I

FOLLOWING IS AN ARTIST CONCEPTION OF THE HIJACKER WHO EXTORTED $200,000 FROM NORTHWEST AIRLINES ON NOVEMBER 24, 1971.

THIS MAN IS DESCRIBED AS FOLLOWS:

RACE . . . . WHITE
SEX . . . . MALE
AGE . . . . MID 40'S
HEIGHT . . . . 5' 10'' TO 6'
WEIGHT . . . . 170 TO 180 POUNDS
BUILD . . . . AVERAGE TO WELL BUILT
COMPLEXION . . . . . OLIVE, LATIN APPERANCE, MEDIUM SMOOTH
HAIR . . . . DARK BROWN OR BLACK, NORMAL STYLE, PARTED ON LEFT, COMBED BACK; SIDEBURNS, LOW EAR LEVEL POSSIBLY BROWN. DURING LATTER PA[...]
EYES . . . . PUT ON DARK, WRAP-AROUND SUNGLAS[...] DRAK RIMS
VOICE . . . . LOW, SPOKE INTELLIGENTLY; NO PA[...] POSSIBLY FROM MIDWEST SECTION O[...]
CHARACTERISTICS . . . HEAVY SMOKER OF RALEIGH FILTER [...]
WEARING APPAREL . . . BLACK SUIT; WHITE SHIRT; NARROW DRESS SUIT; BLACK RAIN-TYPE OVE[...] TOP COAT; DARK BRIEFCASE OR AT[...] RIED PAPER BAG 4" X 12" X 14";

The quiet man in his forties boarded Northwest Orient Airlines Flight 305 from Portland, Oregon, to Seattle, Washington. During the flight, Cooper handed a flight attendant a note saying he had a bomb in his briefcase. He demanded $200,000 and four parachutes. When the plane landed in Seattle, he exchanged the flight's 36 passengers for the **ransom**.

The authorities issued this "wanted" poster featuring artist sketches of Cooper.

Mystery words...

ransom: a sum of money paid for the release of a captive or captives

Cooper Disappears

Cooper told the crew to fly to Mexico City. Somewhere along the way, he jumped from the airplane with a parachute and the money. The pilots landed in Reno, Nevada, but the hijacker was never found.

An investigation found no trace of Cooper. It was assumed he died during the jump. Then, in 1980, a young boy found $5,800 in $20 bills when he was digging a fire pit in Washington state. The bills matched serial numbers from the ransom. Could this mean that Cooper got away with it, after all?

Mystery File:
A FATAL JUMP?

Cooper jumped from the airplane in winter, at night, during a rainstorm. Parachuting into woods at night would be difficult. His parachute could not be steered, and his clothing was not suitable. Most people believe Cooper could not have survived the jump.

Escape from
ALCATRAZ

The prison on Alcatraz Island in San Francisco Bay was said to have been impossible to escape from. In 1962, however, three men did escape on a raft. No one knows what became of them.

The escape took over a year to plan. The men used spoons to loosen concrete around air vents in their cells. They replaced the vents with cardboard. They covered papier-mâché heads with hair and made a raft from rubber raincoats.

The escapers: brothers Clarence (left) and John Anglin (center), and Frank Morris (right).

On the 50th anniversary of the escape, a rumor circulated that the three men would hold a reunion on the island. No one knows where the story began. U.S. marshals spent the day on the island in case the rumor was true--but the inmates never turned up.

Alcatraz is no longer a prison. Today it is a tourist attraction.

On the night of June 11, 1962, the three **inmates** used the fake heads to make it look as if they were asleep in bed. They then escaped through the vents. They got past the guards and climbed over the fences to reach the bay. Then they set out on their homemade raft.

A Possible Sighting

The raft later washed up on the shore, empty. Nearly a month later, a Norwegian ship reported seeing a body in prison clothing floating in the water. Many people believe the three men managed to make it to shore. They may still be at large today.

Mystery words...

inmates: people held captive inside a prison

The Vanishing
VILLAGE

Anjikuni was a remote Inuit community in Kivalliq, Nunavut, Canada. In 1930 a visitor found the entire village deserted. The villagers' disappearance remains unsolved—although some people say that the entire story is a hoax.

The Inuit in northern Canada live in remote villages such as Anjikuni.

Anjikuni was home to about 30 men, women, and children. When a fur trapper named Joe Laballe visited in November 1930, the village was empty. Stew had burned on a fire that still smoldered, so he believed the people must have left quickly. They had not taken any rifles, furs, or food. Laballe was spooked. He traveled to a nearby telegraph office to send a message to the Royal Canadian Mounted Police.

This artist's impression shows "ghost" houses beside Anjikuni Lake.

Disturbed Graves

When the Mounties reached the village, they soon found odd signs. Someone had disturbed nearby graves, removing the bodies. Disturbing a grave was **taboo** for the Inuit. Sled dogs had starved to death, even though the village had plenty of food. The Mounties sent out search parties, but the villagers had vanished. Some people said they had been taken by aliens. Others said that the whole story was made up by Laballe and the journalist who first reported it.

Mystery File:
ALIEN ABDUCTION

Many people claim to have been taken by aliens. In November 1975, Arizona logger Travis Walton disappeared for five days. When he turned up again, he claimed to have been taken to a spaceship by aliens with large eyes. The story has inspired several books and a movie.

Mystery words...

taboo: something that is unacceptable in a society's values

Amelia EARHART

Amelia Earhart was a adventurous American pilot whose feats of aviation captured the public imagination. In 1937, she disappeared in the Pacific during an around-the-world flight. What became of Earhart and her copilot has never been fully confirmed.

Amelia Earhart prepares to board her Lockheed Model 10 Electra.

Amelia Mary Earhart was born in Kansas on July 24, 1897. After learning to fly in the early 1920s, she became the first woman to cross the Atlantic in 1928. The book she wrote about the flight made her famous. In the 1930s, Earhart made a series of pioneering flights. She helped other women be taken seriously as aviators.

Earhart held many records, such as making the first flight from Hawaii to California.

Final Flight

In 1937 Earhart and **navigator** Fred Noonan began a flight around the world. They were about two-thirds into their journey when the plane disappeared over the Pacific Ocean on July 2. Many people believe that the aircraft ditched, or made an emergency landing at sea, and the pair drowned. Others believe they landed on a remote island. In the 1940s, a skeleton was found on nearby Gardner Island. It was never identified, and the bones were later lost. The mystery of Amelia Earhart's disappearance continues to fascinate people today.

Mystery File:
EARHART'S FATE

Some people suggest Earhart moved to New Jersey, where she lived as a housewife under the name Irene Craigmile Bolam. Some think she was captured by the Japanese. Others continue to search the South Sea islands for answers to the mystery.

Mystery words...

navigator: a person who maps the route of a journey

Robin HOOD

The character of Robin Hood has appeared in many books, plays, and movies.

Robin Hood is a legendary bandit who fought for the rights of the poor in England's Sherwood Forest. People told stories about him as long ago as the 14th century—but did he ever really exist?

Old songs and poems tell how Robin Hood and his **outlaw** band, the "Merry Men," outwitted the greedy Sheriff of Nottingham.

In 1225 court records in England mention an **outlaw** named Robert Hod or Hode. Later, names such as Robehod, Hobbehod, or Robynhod were often used for criminals. They did not refer to specific individuals.

The outlaws are said to have hidden deep in Sherwood Forest, a woodland in central England.

Behind the Legend

By the 1600s, scholars were trying to identify the real individual who began the legend. Candidates included a nobleman's son whose property had been seized by the authorities, and an outlaw named Robert of Weatherby. Another possibility was David, Earl of Huntingdon, a noble who rebeled against King John. However, the most likely Robin was Robin, Earl of Loxley. He was loyal to King Richard the Lionheart in the reign of Richard's brother, King John.

Many people believe that Robin Hood is only a legend. The story has stood the test of time, however. It still inspires books, movies, and TV shows.

Mystery File:

MAID MARIAN

In the legend, Robin Hood's partner was Maid Marian. She does not appear in the early stories. Some people believe she may have been Matilda, daughter of Robert Fitzwalter. Fitzwalter led a revolt of the barons against King John.

Mystery words...

outlaw: a person who has broken the law but has not been captured

Malaysia Airlines
FLIGHT 370

In March 2014 a Malaysian airliner with 239 people on board vanished without a trace on a flight from Malaysia to China. A long search over a wide area found nothing. Some believe the plane crashed or was attacked by terrorists. Others believe it landed safely.

Malaysia Airlines Flight 370

△ Navigational waypoint   M765   Air route

1. 00:41 Departs KLIA
2. 01:07 Final ACARS message
3. 01:21 Disappears from secondary radar at waypoint IGARI
4. 02:22 Disappears from military radar

This map shows where the aircraft left its intended route (3).

Malaysia Airlines Flight 370 took off from Kuala Lumpur just after midnight on March 8. At 1:07 A.M., its automatic systems reported that it was cruising at an altitude of 35,000 ft (10,700 m). The final voice transmission came at 1:21 A.M. Satellites later showed that at around 8:11 A.M. the plane was over the Indian Ocean. It was a long way off its original route, but no one knows why it changed direction.

Unsuccessful Search

The airplane had almost certainly crashed into the southern Indian Ocean. A search began of a huge area of ocean west of Australia. Nothing has ever been found. Various theories suggest the plane was a victim of human error, mechanical failure, hijacking, or terrorism.

Mystery File:
THE BLACK BOX

In April 2014, an Australian ship searching for Flight 370 picked up signals that might have been from the plane's "black box," or flight recorder. Robot submarines searched the seabed but found nothing. The fate of the plane and those on board may never be known.

Mystery words...

flight recorder: a device that records information about a flight

Glossary

colony A settlement started in a new country by people from another country

DNA A chemical code passed from parents to their children and from which parentage can be identified

fate Something that is destined to happen to someone

flight recorder A device that records information about a flight

hieroglyphs Picture symbols used in some forms of writing

hijacked Illegally seized an airliner, ship, or vehicle on a journey and made it go to a different destination

historian Someone who studies the past

hoax Something that is deliberately made up to deceive someone

illegitimate Born to parents who are not married

imposter Someone who claims to be somebody else

inmates People held captive inside a prison for crimes

log An official record of events during a voyage or a period of duty

navigator A person who maps the route of a journey

outlaw A person who has broken the law but has not been captured

pretender A person who claims a throne or other high position

ransom A sum of money paid for the release of a captive or captives

satellite A communications device that orbits the Earth

tablet A flat piece of wood or stone used for writing on

taboo Something that is unacceptable in a society's values

telegram A long-distance message sent by telegraph

tsar The emperor of Russia

Find Out More

BOOKS

Clay, Kathryn. *Top 10 Unsolved Mysteries* (Top 10 Unexplained). Capstone Press, 2012.

Hamilton, Sue. *Air and Sea Mysteries* (Unsolved Mysteries). Abdo Publishing Company, 2007.

Hyde, Natalie. *Alcatraz* (Crabtree Chrome). Crabtree Publishing, 2013.

Lusted, Marcia Amidon. *The D. B. Cooper Hijacking* (Unsolved Mysteries). Essential Library, 2012.

Storrie, Paul, and Thomas Yeates. *Robin Hood: Outlaw of Sherwood Forest* (Graphic Myths and Legends). Graphic Universe, 2006.

WEBSITES

History's Greatest Unsolved
A directory of the world's greatest unsolved mysteries.
http://list25.com/25-greatest-unsolved-mysteries-ever/

Amelia Earhart
The aviator's official website, with full details of her life
www.ameliaearhart.com/

Robin Hood
The Robin Hood Society introduces the many faces of the outlaw.
www.robinhood.ltd.uk/

Index